IMAGES
of America

SAN DIEGO
HARBOR POLICE

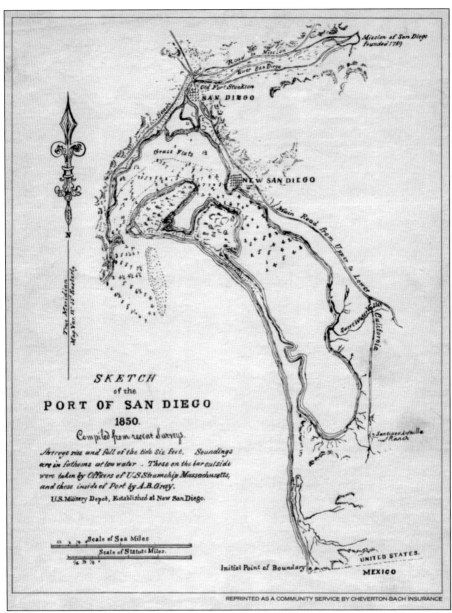

SKETCH
of the
PORT OF SAN DIEGO
1850.

Compiled from recent Surveys.

Average rise and fall of the tide six feet. Soundings
are in fathoms at low water. These on the bar outside
were taken by Officers of U.S. Steamship Massachusetts,
and those inside of Port by A.B. Gray.

U.S. Military Depot, Established at New San Diego.

Scale of Sea Miles
Scale of Statute Miles.

MAP OF SAN DIEGO BAY, 1850. San Diego Bay is a natural harbor and deepwater port located in San Diego County, California. San Diego Bay is 12 miles (19 kilometers) long and varies between one and three miles (1.6 to 4.8 kilometers) wide. San Diego Bay is the third largest of the three protected natural bays on California. (Courtesy of F.W. Wittich Sr. family.)

ON THE COVER: The San Diego Harbor Police Department is the premier police presence on San Diego Bay, at the San Diego International Airport, and on all tidelands around the bay. Their jurisdiction extends throughout five member cities of the Port District, which include San Diego, Chula Vista, Coronado, Imperial Beach, and National City. (Courtesy of the San Diego Maritime Museum.)

IMAGES
of America

SAN DIEGO
HARBOR POLICE

Michael P. Rich

ARCADIA
PUBLISHING

Published by Arcadia Publishing
Charleston, South Carolina

Printed in the United States of America

Library of Congress Control Number: 2014936978

For all general information, please contact Arcadia Publishing:
Telephone 843-853-2070
Fax 843-853-0044
E-mail sales@arcadiapublishing.com
For customer service and orders:
Toll-Free 1-888-313-2665

Visit us on the Internet at www.arcadiapublishing.com

This book is dedicated to those early Harbor Police officers whose dedication and service to their country during World War II formed the department into what it is today. Sweat and perseverance is what their heroic generation was made of. The Harbor Police will always be in gratitude to men such as Chief Ellsworth Kiser, Chief Edgar Taylor, and Chief Arthur LeBlanc—men who overcame all of the odds to come home, serve their country, and protect life and property in America's finest city.

*"Freedom is never more than one generation away from extinction.
We didn't pass it to our children in the bloodstream. It must be fought
for, protected, and handed on for them to do the same."*

—Ronald Reagan

SAN DIEGO HARBOR POLICE HEADQUARTERS. This building is located on Harbor Drive in the city of San Diego. (Courtesy of the San Diego Unified Port District.)

CONTENTS

ACKNOWLEDGMENTS

I would like thank those people who contributed photographs and information vital to the documentation of the history of the San Diego Harbor Police. This book would not have been possible if it were not for the families of Harbor Police officers, past and present. Special thanks go to Richard Kiser, the son of Chief Ellsworth Kiser, for his contribution of photographs and early memorabilia that document the service of his father and the early years of the Harbor Police. Thanks to Barbara Wittich, who provided photographs of her father, Frank Wittich, one of the first Harbor Police officers from the early years of the department. Both the Harbor Police and the author were honored to be visited by John Riddle, the grandson of John C. Riddle, who contributed photographs of his grandfather. This historical project would not have been possible without the support of San Diego Harbor police chief John Bolduc, assistant chief Mark Stainbrook, Lt. Dominick Boccia, San Diego assistant chief of police Todd Jarvis, retired Oceanside police chief Don Hadley, and the officers of the Harbor Police—their support and contribution of departmental photographs made this book a reality. Thanks also go to Kevin Sheehan—librarian for the San Diego Maritime Museum—who was instrumental in providing several historic photographs and research on San Diego Bay. I would like to thank the first female Harbor Police officer, Linda Knoebel, and Harbor Police officer Sherrie Pfohl for their valuable assistance and photographs for this publication.

This book would not have been possible were it not for the support of the San Diego Unified Port District, including Dale Frost, Marguerite Elicone, and Arash Afshar.

SAN DIEGO HARBOR. This view of the harbor in 1905 features a French cruiser; the battleship USS *Wyoming*, built by the Union Iron Works in San Francisco, in April 1899; the USS *Chicago*, a protected cruiser that was built by William Cramp & Sons in Philadelphia, Pennsylvania, in June 1888; and the *Manning*, a revenue cutter of the USRC, which served from 1898 to 1930 and saw service in the US Navy during the Spanish-American war. (Courtesy of the San Diego Unified Port District.)

INTRODUCTION

San Diego's rich history is based on its connection to its naturally formed deepwater harbor. Portuguese explorer Juan Rodriguez Cabrillo discovered California by sailing into what is now San Diego Bay in 1542, thus claiming the harbor and surrounding region for the king of Spain.

In the year 1769, the first European settlement was formed in San Diego when Franciscan fathers established a mission on a hill overlooking San Diego Bay. The Franciscans settled next to a large Native American village. This area, known as Old Town, became a thriving village by the 1880s and was a vital shipping port. San Diego Harbor was, by then, becoming a bustling port where ships loaded and unloaded cattle, hides, and quarried stone.

In 1822, Mexico achieved independence from Spain, and San Diego became the capital of Mexican California. In 1846—after the Mexican-American War—the US Army established permanent American rule over San Diego, which was incorporated in 1850.

San Diego Harbor transitioned into a vital whaling port and a base for fur trading on the West Coast. In 1867, San Francisco land developer Alonzo E. Horton bought a 1,000-acre plot of land that later became downtown San Diego. Horton was instrumental in laying out the city's streets and built San Diego's first wharf and hotel, along San Diego Harbor. Now that the city of San Diego had a growing population, residents found that a larger police force was vital to the city's success. Prior to 1889, law enforcement in San Diego was handled by a group of city marshals and constables, consisting of patrolmen, a detective, a criminologist, a jailor, a process server, clerk, and an executioner.

In 1870, the California gold rush began and ignited a land boom in San Diego—increasing the population to 40,000. With the arrival of the Santa Fe Railroad, the country became connected to San Diego and its harbor. In 1850, the City of San Diego built the first town jail at a cost of $5,000. In 1871, a new jail was established on the site of the present-day county courthouse, at Front and C Streets. Finally, on May 16, 1889, the San Diego Police Department was established and named its first police chief, Joseph Coyne.

As the boom of the 1880s lured new settlers, San Diego Harbor prospered as well. As legend has it, the Stingaree District was formed when sailors came into San Diego Bay after long trips and would traverse the shallows of San Diego Bay in order to debark in the newly developing downtown area of San Diego. As the sailors traversed the shallows, they were often stung by stingrays, and so the name Stingaree was applied to the gas lamp quarter of San Diego. In the 1880s, this area was dominated by brothels, drug dens, and gambling halls, as well as the criminals who provided these illegal activities to sailors and other visitors. At the time, local law enforcement mostly overlooked the area, and residents learned to stay away from the district.

In the mid-1880s, Wyatt Earp moved to San Diego, where he owned and operated three gambling halls in the Stingaree. The Stingaree also encompassed San Diego's Chinatown, many inhabitants of which worked on fishing boats and the railroads.

In 1915, San Diego hosted the Panama-California Exposition to celebrate the completion of the Panama Canal. This upcoming exposition required city officials to clean up the Stingaree district, resulting in police raids of the area. The exposition boosted the aircraft industry in San Diego, and, in 1927, Charles A. Lindbergh made San Diego the starting point for the first-ever flight of his famous plane, the *Spirit of St. Louis*. Lindbergh later agreed to lend his name to San Diego's new airport, the San Diego Municipal Airport—Lindbergh Field. The new airport was located on Pacific Highway and was built up with mud dredged from San Diego Bay. In 1919, the San Diego Harbor Commission and Harbor Department were established to administer the tidelands area.

As San Diego faced the outbreak of World War II, the military developed Lindbergh Field into a modern aviation transportation center. The US Army Air Corps took over the airport in

1942, and Army engineers improved the existing runways to accommodate the heavy bombers that were manufactured in San Diego. The US Navy chose San Diego Harbor as an alternate base after Japan's bombing of Pearl Harbor. Additionally, San Diego Harbor became the home of the San Diego Naval Training Center (NTC). Along with the military presence, related support industries and a large number of naval and aviation defense contractors sprang up on San Diego Bay. The US military maintained control of the San Diego Harbor until 1948, when it returned the responsibilities of law enforcement and bay security to the City of San Diego.

SAN DIEGO HARBOR. On July 9, 1938, a Japanese training ship and the aircraft carrier USS *Ranger* CV-4 were moored at NAS North Island, in San Diego. Commissioned on June 4, 1934, the *Ranger* saw extensive service in World War II. (Courtesy of the San Diego Unified Port District.)

LINDBERGH FIELD, 1928. This photograph shows large crowds gathered for an air show on the packed-mud landing field. (Courtesy of the San Diego Unified Port District.)

One

SAN DIEGO

HARBOR DIVISION

THE EARLY DAYS

1948–1962

Due to the growing population of San Diego, the San Diego Police Department formed the Security Division. The Security Division was responsible for patrolling the 1,800 acres of tidelands that were used in commerce, navigation, and fishing.

At the close of World War II, when the Port of San Diego was returned to local control by the military, it was deemed necessary to establish security on the tidelands, docks, and piers owned by the City of San Diego. A start was made in 1948, with two wharfingers, a chief of Harbor Police, five patrolmen, and two guards assigned to the municipal airport. The wharfingers worked from 8:00 a.m. to 5:00 p.m. and were primarily used to check in cargo and service ships. The two men assigned to the airport worked day watches only, and at night the airport was checked periodically by the San Diego Police Department. The classification of the patrolmen assigned to the tidelands was "Guards, Harbor and Lakes."

In 1954, when great quantities of cotton began to accumulate on the waterfront for shipment overseas, a port security force was established. This force was led by the port warden, who was charged with the safety and well-being of the port. The warden was assisted by three sergeants and 16 patrolmen. The Municipal Airport was then covered 24 hours a day by port security. The patrol and security of the municipal yacht harbor was handled by the harbormaster and a Port Security officer. Until 1954, the San Diego Bay relied on the fireboat *Bill Kettner* for firefighting responsibilities. The *Bill Kettner* was built in 1919, served the San Diego bay area for many years, and was crewed by San Diego fire personnel who, during World War II, were assisted by US Navy personnel.

In early 1957, in order to upgrade the quality of training for Port Security officers, the first officer attended and graduated from the San Diego Police Academy. Since that date, all officers have been required to attend a Certified Peace Officer Academy in the state of California. Boating began to boom in the mid-1950s and it was necessary to concentrate more and more on traffic control and safety on the waters of the bay. In 1959, the position of harbormaster was abolished, and a Port Security sergeant was assigned—along with four patrolmen. In 1960, the Port Security force was revised, with the wharfingers being assigned to the marine terminal operation forming the Harbor Patrol Division.

HARBOR SECURITY DIVISION OFFICER. Officer Frank Wittich watches the construction of Harbor Island. Harbor Island is a man-made peninsula, created in 1961 from harbor dredgings. Harbor Island is two miles long and only a few hundred feet wide. (Courtesy of San Diego Unified Port District.)

PERSONS ARRESTED IN SAN DIEGO FOR DRUNKENESS
(Exclusive of driving while drunk)

1934-35
5,998

1935-36
8,214

1936-37
7,895

1937-38
6,638

1938-39
6,301

EACH COMPLETED FIGURE REPRESENTS 1,000 ARRESTS

CITY ARRESTS. This 1934 City of San Diego Fiscal Report publication shows the yearly arrests for public drunkenness, between 1934 and 1939. (Courtesy of the San Diego Unified Port District.)

1934 FISCAL REPORT. This 1934 fiscal report shows the monthly retirement fund rates for fire and police officers in San Diego. (Courtesy of San Diego Unified Port District.)

2¼ cents went for

Retirement Funds

- Average monthly city employees pension $45.67
- Average monthly police employees pension. . . . $94.01
- Average monthly fire employees pension $97.20
- Per capita cost Retirement Funds 1938-39 . . . . . $ 0.59

CITY EMPLOYEES' RETIREMENT
Required 1½c of the Tax Dollar

Personnel 1
Municipal employees (except Fire and Police), elective officers and members of Commissions come within the provisions of the City Employees' Retirement System. The system is supported by joint contributions of the city and employee, not to exceed five per cent of the employee's salary, depending upon age of entrance into the system. Retirement of employees is optional after ten years of continuous service provided age 62 has been attained, and mandatory at the age of 72. Administration of the funds is under control of a board of seven members.

During the past fiscal year six persons were retired on pensions, six died; bringing the total now receiving pensions to 105. A total of 865 members are shown on the rolls of the Retirement System, the total assets of which are $1,118,576.12.
Expenditures 1938-39 . . . . $68,571.91   Per Capita . . . .36⅝c.

POLICE RETIREMENT
Required 4 Mills of the Tax Dollar

The Police Retirement Fund received approximately 70% of its money from the City last year, i.e., 35% from 1/3 of court fines, 5½% from a twentieth of the amounts received for Municipal licenses and 29% from the City contributing an amount equal to the employees' contributions. The fund showed a deficit for the year of $5,924.93. This condition might be alleviated if the system was set up on an actuarial basis.

During the past fiscal year seven men were retired on pensions, three men died and two widows were added to the rolls, bringing the total

BADGE. This photograph shows a c. 1948 San Diego Harbor Police chief's badge. (Courtesy of Michael P. Rich.)

FIRE VESSEL BILL KETTNER. Photographed in 1934, the *Bill Kettner's* seven-man fire crew stands by in San Diego Bay. The *Bill Kettner* served San Diego Bay from 1919 until the late 1950s. The tug was 65 feet long, and had a beam of 18 feet. The vessel was equipped with a 220 horsepower Atlas engine and two 110 Seagrave engines for pumping. The fire tug had a speed of 10 knots and threw 6,000 gallons of water per minute. The *Bill Kettner* is now privately owned. (Photo courtesy of the San Diego Maritime Museum.)

HARBOR SECURITY DIVISION, 1958. The Harbor Patrol Division officers were employed by the City of San Diego until the formation of the port district in 1962. Seen here, from left to right, are; Capt. Richard Storm, Port Warden J. Murtha, Sgt. Ellsworth Kiser, Sgt. E. Thomas, Sgt. W. Clifford, and Pier Supervisor J. Poukkula. (Photo Courtesy of Richard Kiser.)

HARBORMASTER. The harbormaster is seen here on a security and safety patrol—off of Broadway Pier—in 1954. (Courtesy of San Diego Unified Port District.)

HARBOR SECURITY DIVISION OFFICER ASSISTING BOATER. On September 25, 1953, an officer throws a line to a boater stranded off of Point Loma. Each Harbor Division officer was required to be proficient in basic boating skills, including knot tying and line handling. (Courtesy of San Diego Unified Port District.)

Cargo Ship Unloading. On July 27, 1959, the cargo ship *Delfino* unloaded sheep onto the 10th Avenue Marine Terminal. The cargo terminal was equipped with cattle and sheep holding yards, for both imported and exported livestock. (Courtesy of San Diego Unified Port District.)

On Watch. This Harbor Division Security Division officer checks in at his 10th Avenue Marine Terminal time clock. (Courtesy of San Diego Unified Port District.)

GATE DUTY. This Harbor Security Division officer maintains a watch over the main gate at the 10th Avenue Marine Shipping Terminal, on February 17, 1959. In 2013, San Diego's principal inbound cargoes were refrigerated commodities, fertilizer, cement, and forest products. The primary export cargoes included refrigerated cargo and bulk commodities. Currently, the Dole Fresh Fruit Company imports 185 million bananas every month through the terminal. (Courtesy of San Diego Unified Port District.)

POINT LOMA. Pictured in 1959, the Point Loma Sport Fishing stand was located at 1403 Scott Street. The sport fishing industry plays a major role in San Diego history. In February 1936, the San Diego Sport Fisherman's Association was formed. When World War II broke out, some of the vessels in the H&M fleet were put into service as military transports and supply craft. In 1952, Lee Palm bought the sport fisher fleet and began an "organized" approach to pioneering long range sport fishing from H&M. (Courtesy of San Diego Unified Port District.)

FIRE TRAINING. Photographed in 1959, these Harbor Division officers proudly stand in their fire gear during firefighting training at the 32nd Street Naval Base. Harbor Division officers were originally issued surplus US Navy fire protective gear. (Courtesy of San Diego Unified Port District Archives.)

FIRE LINE HANDLING. In 1959, Harbor Division officers practice fire hose line handling. San Diego Harbor Police officers are currently required to attend a certified Marine firefighting school and carry personal protective firefighting gear with them on patrol at all times. (Courtesy of San Diego Unified Port District.)

HARBOR DIVISION DIVER, 1958.
Diver Glenn Orr prepares to
enter the waters of San Diego
Bay, off the patrol vessel *Point
Loma* at the Harbor Division
office on Shelter Island. Post
World War II, new scuba tank
technology was developed and,
in 1952, the Cousteau-designed
aqualungs reached markets in the
United States. (Courtesy of San
Diego Unified Port District.)

**REGULATION DIVING GEAR,
1958.** Glenn Orr poses for a
photo on Shelter Island and is
displaying his issued scuba fins,
mask, and tank. (Courtesy of San
Diego Unified Port District.)

SAN DIEGO HARBOR SECURITY DIVISION, 1959. The division stands proud in front of the Harbor Division station, located on Shelter Island. At this point, the division consisted of 19 officers, 4 sergeants, and a captain. The assistant harbormaster is pictured in the dark blue uniform. Several men from the security force were designated as assistant harbormasters and adopted dark blue uniforms with a nautical design. Harbor Division officers wore dark-green wool pants, and tan wool-blend shirts. (Courtesy of Richard Kiser.)

HARBOR DIVISION VESSEL *POINT LOMA II.* Built in 1957, this dual-purpose fire and patrol vessel served until 1976. Here, the vessel is shown speeding through North San Diego Bay on October 21, 1960—piloted by Officer Frank Wittich. (Courtesy of F.W. Wittich Sr. family.)

SHELTER ISLAND LAUNCH RAMP. In 1957, weekend traffic jams were a regular occurrence at Shelter Island, as hundreds of outboards were launched from the ramp. (Courtesy of San Diego Unified Port District.)

HARBOR DIVISION
OFFICER ON FOOT PATROL.
Photographed in 1959, this
division officer patrols the
area of G Street Pier and
Harbor Drive. Tom Lai's
Chinese Restaurant gave
way to the Fish Market
Restaurant in the 1960s.
(Courtesy of San Diego
Unified Port District.)

HENRY CABOT LODGE

October 22, 1960

Dear Lieutenant Kiser:

Please accept this expression of my sincere
thanks for the tremendously hard and effective work
which you did in connection with my recent visit.
It was in every way a memorable occasion and I con-
gratulate you on the splendid arrangements which you
made.

I was delighted to have had this chance to
visit with you, and I do hope that our paths will
cross again before too long.

If ever I can be of any possible assistance
in the future, please don't hesitate to call upon me.

With renewed thanks and with best wishes,

Sincerely,

Henry Cabot Lodge

Henry Cabot Lodge

Lieutenant Elsworth Kiser
1365 North Harbor Drive
San Diego, California

APPRECIATION LETTER.
This letter was written to
Harbor Division lieutenant
Ellsworth Kiser, by Henry
Cabot Lodge, on October
22nd 1960. Henry Cabot
Lodge was a Republican
senator and historian from
Massachusetts. Lodge
was a friend of Theodore
Roosevelt and was the first
senate majority leader.
(Courtesy of Richard Kiser.)

HARBORMASTER AND ASSISTANTS. Here, equipment is demonstrated for a film crew aboard the patrol vessel *Point Loma*. In 1957, San Diego Harbor Division boats and Port District piers and wharfs were often used for filming the TV series *Harbor Command*, which was produced by Metro-Goldwyn-Mayer Studios and starred Wendall Corey as Capt. Ralph Baxter. (Courtesy of San Diego Unified Port District.)

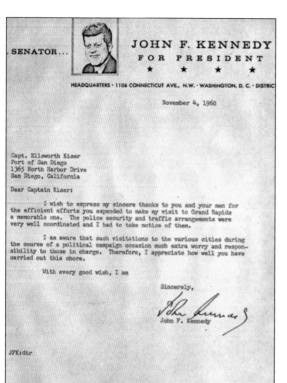

November 4, 1960

Capt. Ellsworth Kiser
Port of San Diego
1365 North Harbor Drive
San Diego, California

Dear Captain Kiser:

I wish to express my sincere thanks to you and your men for the efficient efforts you expended to make my visit to Grand Rapids a memorable one. The police security and traffic arrangements were very well coordinated and I had to take notice of them.

I am aware that such visitations to the various cities during the course of a political campaign occasion much extra worry and responsibility to those in charge. Therefore, I appreciate how well you have carried out this chore.

With every good wish, I am

Sincerely,

John F. Kennedy

JFK:dtr

LETTER OF APPRECIATION. This letter was written to Capt. Ellsworth Kiser from presidential candidate John F. Kennedy, on November 4, 1960. John Fitzgerald Kennedy served as the 35th president of the United States, from January 1961 until he was assassinated in November 1963. (Courtesy of Richard Kiser.)

MISS PORT OF SAN DIEGO. Gathering attention from the docked cargo ship sailors, Miss Port of San Diego poses for a photo shoot on a cotton bale. (Courtesy of San Diego Unified Port District.)

Patrol Vessel Shelter Island. On May 25, 1961, the Port of San Diego's newest fire and patrol vessel was launched at the Kettenburg Boat Works. Kettenburg Marine is still located at 2500 Shelter Island Drive and holds a place in San Diego's boating history. (Courtesy of San Diego Unified Port District.)

Harbor Division Vehicle. Pictured here in 1962, Officer Willie Jinright stands in front of a vehicle while displaying standardized safety equipment—consisting of flares, an oxygen bottle, strobes, and a life ring. Up until 1963, Port of San Diego vehicles used the official seal of the City of San Diego. (Courtesy of San Diego Unified Port District.)

SAN DIEGO POLICE ACADEMY GRADUATION. San Diego Harbor Policeman William S. Hall (first row, seventh officer from the left) was one of four harbor policemen in this academy class. William Hall retired from the US Navy in 1957 as a commander, after 31 years of service. He entered the Navy at age 17 as an E-1 and rose through the ranks, becoming a warrant officer and eventually receiving a commission prior to the start of World War II. He was a World War II and Korean War veteran. In late 1957, William Hall was hired as a harbormaster and then found himself attending the San Diego police academy when the Port District was formed in 1963. He was 55 years old when he graduated from the academy in January 1964. While attending the academy, he attained the highest academic scores and was voted "Honor Man" by his class of 55 recruits. He retired from the Port District in the early 1970s. Officer Hall's grandson Todd Jarvis is currently an assistant chief of police for the San Diego Police Department. (Courtesy of William S. Hall family.)

Two

THE SAN DIEGO HARBOR POLICE
THE DEPARTMENT TRANSITIONS

As the fourth largest of the 11 ports in California, it was becoming apparent that it was necessary to form a separate agency to watch over and maintain the Port of San Diego. The San Diego Unified Port District was created when the California State Legislature approved Senate Bill 41, which was certified by the County Board of Supervisors in 1962. With the formation of the Unified Port District in 1963, the present Harbor Police force came into being.

The new police force was renamed the San Diego Harbor Police Department. This new department was responsible for policing and firefighting on nearly 6,000 acres—half land and half water. The Harbor Police Department has jurisdiction over the tidelands areas in five member cities: Chula Vista, Coronado, Imperial Beach, National City, and San Diego. The Board of Port Commissioners, by resolution, required that Harbor Police meet the minimum standards for peace officers set by California state law. This required the department to raise standards for the entrance examination and provide additional training. The entrance qualifications were made comparable to those for the deputy sheriff of San Diego County, and training was intensified to meet additional duties.

In 1963, the San Diego Unified Port Commissioners named Harbor Division captain Ellsworth Kiser as the first San Diego Harbor Police's chief of police. Ellsworth Kiser had joined the Harbor Division in 1956 after retiring from the Navy as a boatswain's mate. Ellsworth Kiser, having served in both World War II and Korea, had tremendous boating knowledge and quickly worked his way through the ranks.

A HELPING HAND. Harbor Police officer Willie A. Jinright and Chief Ellsworth Kiser's son Richard interact in this photograph, taken on August 15, 1962. (Courtesy of Richard Kiser.)

SAN DIEGO UNIFIED PORT DISTRICT EMBLEM. On December 12, 1963, a new emblem is placed over the City of San Diego Seal on this Harbor Police vehicle. (Courtesy of San Diego Unified Port District.)

CHIEF ELLSWORTH KISER. Ellsworth Kiser served the San Diego Harbor Police from 1956 until his sudden death on June 7, 1974. Chief Kiser was instrumental in the forming of the San Diego Harbor Police. (Courtesy of San Diego Unified Port District.)

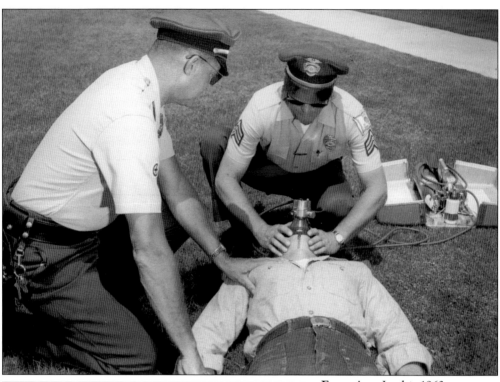

FIRST AID. In this 1963 photograph, Harbor Police sergeant William Clifford and Officer Guy Davis demonstrate their life saving skills while using a new lightweight resuscitator. In 1963, all Harbor Police officers were required to have an advanced first aid certification and an FCC radio operators' permit, in addition to normal police academy training. (Courtesy of Richard Kiser.)

PORT OF SAN DIEGO

INTER-DEPARTMENTAL COMMUNICATION

DATE: 7 February 1963

TO: E. KISER, Chief, Harbor Patrol

FROM: JOHN BATE, Port Director

SUBJECT: Cleaning of Watch Stations

I have reviewed your Patrol Report dated 29 January relative to the cleaning of the traffic control center at the Tenth Avenue Marine Terminal and have asked Mr. Moural and Mr. Liebmann to examine the janitorial requirements of the South Gate at the airport and this watch station.

It is recognized that the watch station at Shelter Island must be maintained at very high standards; however, in reviewing the other two stations, it would seem to me that ex-Navy men would utilize a bit of Windex, a broom, and other utensils to keep those two watch stations clean. I have never seen anyone there particularly overburdened with duties that would prohibit this.

Will you kindly make the necessary arrangements, therefore, to have these men on watch take care of these two stations. The cost of providing janitorial services at these two stations is prohibitive and, in my opinion, unnecessary.

JOHN BATE

JB/ef

POLICE STATION CLEANING LETTER. New Harbor Police chief Ellsworth Kiser once asked Port Director Bate for cleaning service at the Harbor Police station in this letter. The port director had a very direct response for the new chief, as seen left. (Courtesy of Richard Kiser.)

SHELTER ISLAND STATION. Harbor Police officer Deforest Schoeman broadcasts to units in the harbor from the base station radio. (Courtesy of the San Diego Unified Port District.)

AIRPORT DUTY. Here, Harbor Police officer B.T. Morris demonstrates that duty at Lindbergh Field Airport involves answering a lot of questions. Officer Morris helps Mr. and Mrs. Jack Fruhling of Long Island, New York. Obviously, children's car seats did not require the same safety standards in 1963. (Courtesy of the San Diego Unified Port District.)

Line Handling Skills. Officers Willie Jinright and John Hackbarth demonstrate how to tie a bowline knot on the vessel *Point Loma*, on July 30, 1963. (Courtesy of the San Diego Unified Port District.)

BAY WATCH.
Pictured here in 1966, Capt. Edgar Taylor and Sgt. William Hall are stationed in the Harbor Control building on Shelter Island. Capt. Taylor is observing a boat entering San Diego Bay, and Sgt. Hall is dispatching vessel units. (Courtesy San Diego History Center, *Union Tribune* Collection.)

STANDING WATCH. Seen here in 1966, Officer Jack Gobel stands watch and observes boat traffic entering San Diego Bay. The Shelter Island Harbor Police station also served as an office for the US Coast Guard, and the US Departments of Agriculture, Customs, Immigration, and Health. (Courtesy San Diego History Center, *Union Tribune* Collection.)

VEHICLE PATROL. Pictured in 1966, this officer radios in vessel traffic on Shelter Island. In the background are the Harbor Police vessel *Point Loma* and a carrier anchored in North San Diego Bay. (Courtesy San Diego History Center, *Union Tribune* Collection.)

RIOT CONTROL TRAINING. The Watts Riots forever changed law enforcement in Southern California. The riots took place in the Watts neighborhood of Los Angeles, on August 11, 1965. These six days of unrest resulted in 34 deaths, 1,032 injuries, 3,438 arrests, and over $40 million in property damage. The San Diego Harbor Police prepared for future events by conducting riot control drills and issuing helmets to all officers. From 1965 to 1967, it was mandatory for officers to wear helmets while on patrol. (Courtesy of Richard Kiser)

MORE RIOT CONTROL TRAINING. Here, officers drill on Shelter Island in 1965. (Courtesy of Richard Kiser.)

HANDGUN PRACTICE. Officers George Walsh, Leroy Smith, and Claude Stark practice their quick draw skills at the San Diego Police Department pistol range, located at 4008 Federal Boulevard in San Diego. The range was opened in 1931, when San Diego Police Department janitor Ronald Pease got the job of pistol range instructor after he was found to be a crack shot. The five-acre piece of land hosts an 80-foot-long cobblestone clubhouse, built from scavenged material. Since 1931, approximately 8,000 San Diego police officers have trained at the range. (Courtesy of the San Diego Unified Port District.)

HANDGUN FUNCTION DEMONSTRATION. Officers refresh themselves in the function of the Smith & Wesson Model 10 Police Revolver. The weapon fired a .38 caliber, 158-grain bullet. Over 6,000,000 weapons of the type were produced over the years, making it the most popular center fire revolver of the 20th century. The Smith & Wesson revolver was standard issue for the Harbor Police until the early 1980s. (Courtesy of the San Diego Unified Port District.)

Lindbergh Field Airport. April 20, 1964. A lone officer stands post at Terminal 1, located on Pacific Highway. (Courtesy of the San Diego Unified Port District.)

CALIFORNIA GOVERNOR RONALD REAGAN. February 8, 1967. Officer Frank Wittich stands on perimeter security during the arrival of Gov. Ronald Reagan. Gov. Reagan was in San Diego for the dedication of the new Terminal 1 at Lindbergh Field. Located at 3665 North Harbor Drive, Terminal 1 was previously at Pacific Highway. (Courtesy of F.W. Wittich Sr. family.)

RANGE PRACTICE. Quarterly range qualifications were mandatory for officers, with both handguns and shotguns. The officer pictured is qualifying with his model 10 Smith & Wesson revolver, in 1966. (Courtesy of the San Diego Unified Port District.)

AIRPORT DUTY. Officer Julius Harper gives directions to visitors at Lindbergh Field in the winter of 1966. Officer Harper served the Harbor Police until his retirement in the late 1980s. He is seen here wearing one of the early handheld radios made by General Electric. (Courtesy of the San Diego Unified Port District.)

OFFICER FRANK WITTICH. Born April 30, 1918, Officer Wittich served the San Diego Harbor Police until 1973. He served in the US Navy for 25 years before joining the Harbor Police. Wittich was a World War II and Korean War veteran.

Port of San Diego

The Night Before Christmas
at
Harbor Control

T'was the night before Christmas and all thru the
port.
  Not a ship was stirring of any kind or
sort.

  The watch was on station as always before.
Performing their duty without any
pause.

Except Sgt Thomas, who stayed home tonight to see
Santa Claus.

The boats were all hung at the float for the
night
With bow and stern lines all snugged up and
tight.

There was Ballast Pt, Pt Loma and of course the
Zuniga
For all sorts of aid they were ready and
eager.

But the Yachtsmen tonight provided no
action
And the wait for St. Nick was the big
attraction.

From Yacht Harbor Dr. to twenty eighth street
an exceptional quiet hung over the
beat.

The Airport patrol and man at South Gate with not
much to do but stand round and wait

Phone 233-0181

Port of San Diego

Kept their eyes on the skies up toward
Heaven.
In case the Old Gent approached runaway
twenty seven.

But by 0300 he still had'nt shown
So it's a pretty good chance that he's not being
flown.

The watch down at tenth and the duty Wharfinger
Kept check on the docks, the berths and the
slip.
With the hope that Old Santa would come in by
ship.

With the Pilots all sleeping thats rather
remote
So I strongly expect his arrival by
boat.

And if he does, there's one thing I know
It will just be my luck to take him in
tow.

As I hand him the line and turn on my
light
A voice loud and clear rings out in the
night.

Merry Christmas, A Merry Christmas to All and to
All a Good night.

Wittich #7

Phone 233-0181

CHRISTMAS, 1967. Officer Frank Wittich wrote this Christmas poem for the Harbor Police officers and their families. Officer Wittich served the San Diego Harbor Police from 1956 through the early 1970s. (Courtesy of F.W. Wittich Sr. family.)

Three

THE SAN DIEGO HARBOR POLICE

THE 1970S

The 1970s were a time of change for the San Diego Harbor Police, and the city of San Diego. The Harbor Police had transitioned from a sleepy, fourteen-man department to one that was constantly growing and modernizing. The department's officers, whose badges had read "Patrolman," were now being issued new badges reading "Police Officer." The times were changing socially, and, in the coming years, the department would face its biggest challenges—the sudden death of Chief Ellsworth Kiser on June 7, 1974, and the tragic crash of Pacific Southwest Airlines Flight, No. 182.

On the morning of September 25, 1978, San Diego woke up to tragedy. As PSA Flight 182 approached Lindbergh Field from Sacramento, the plane was struck by a single engine Cessna 172. The collision brought an abrupt end to the routine flights for both aircraft. The Cessna spun out of control—crashing and killing both pilots—and the PSA aircraft was critically damaged. With its portside wing ablaze, Flight 182's final transmission was, "Tower, we're going down . . . this is PSA."

Flight 182 crashed 17 seconds later, at 9:02 AM, and 144 lives were ended as the plane struck a North Park neighborhood. The city of San Diego—and the Harbor Police who were on duty at Lindbergh Field—had never witnessed such a tragedy in its history. The impact of the crash caused the ground to shake throughout the city, and a thick black plume of smoke towered hundreds of feet above the city as a signal to San Diegans that tragedy had struck. Within minutes, Harbor Police officers working at Lindbergh Field had to face the realization that one of their returning flights would not be landing, and officers who had witnessed thousands of flights coming and going from the terminal now had to face shocked and distraught families that had been waiting for the return of their loved ones to San Diego. Harbor Police officers on duty gathered distraught families and provided comfort as best as possible, all while controlling the news media that converged on the airport and crash site. As of that date, Flight 182 was the worst air disaster in US history.

RUNWAY OF LINDBERGH FIELD. An officer uses his car radio while patrolling the runway, adjacent to a PSA aircraft. (Courtesy of San Diego Unified Port District.)

Federal Bureau of Investigation
United States Department of Justice
Washington, D. C.

August 21, 1970

Chief Ellsworth Kiser
San Diego Harbor Police
San Diego Port Authority
Post Office Box 488
San Diego, California 92112

My dear Chief:

    I want to thank you for the praiseworthy assistance which you rendered to Mr. Tolson and me during our recent trip to San Diego.

    Your kindness and consideration did much to assure a pleasant visit and I want you to know how much we appreciate the courtesies that were extended to us.

    Sincerely,

J. Edgar Hoover

J. EDGAR HOOVER LETTER. This letter was written to Chief Kiser, in appreciation for a visit to San Diego Bay. John Edgar Hoover was the first director of the Federal Bureau of Investigation of the United States. He passed away on May 2, 1972. (Courtesy of F.W. Wittich Sr. family.)

CORONADO BRIDGE. Opened to traffic on August 3, 1969, the Coronado Bridge is 11,179 feet long and reaches a height of 200 feet—allowing the US Navy ships which operate out of the nearby Naval Base San Diego to pass underneath it. The construction of the bridge marked the ending of the Coronado ferry and a boom in automobile traffic in the 1970s to the city of Coronado. (Courtesy of Officer Kenneth Helman.)

CHIEF EDGAR L. TAYLOR. In July 1974, Harbor Police captain Edgar Taylor was named chief of the Harbor Police. Chief Taylor had served 20 years in the US Navy and, upon retirement in 1955, joined the Harbor Division. Chief Taylor saw combat duty in both World War II and Korea, serving on submarines and battleships. (Courtesy of San Diego Unified Port District.)

Lunch on Shelter Island. In the spring of 1967, Officer Lucian Urbanski greets children on the grass outside of the Shelter Island police station. In the background is the Friendship Bell, which the citizens of Yokohama, Japan presented to San Diego in May 1958. Located at 1401 Shelter Island Drive, the bell stands six feet high and weighs almost two and a half tons. (Courtesy of San Diego Unified Port District.)

John Wayne. Officer Jack Steven (right) poses with John Wayne at the Harbor Police dock on Shelter Island in the summer of 1968. John Wayne was the stage name of Marion Robert Morrison, who was born on May 26, 1907, and worked as an actor, director, and producer. A longtime resident of Southern California, Wayne died in 1979. (Courtesy of Jonathan Hoover.)

BREAK TIME. Officer Jack Steven and his dive partner take a few minutes from their dive training for a coffee and cigarette break in the winter of 1968. (Courtesy of Jonathan Hoover.)

PATROL VESSEL POINT ZUNIGA. This photograph shows the christening of the *Point Zuniga* on June 9, 1973. Mrs. Dudley had the honor of breaking the champagne bottle on the bow of the new patrol vessel. (Courtesy of the San Diego Unified Port District Archives.)

HARBOR POLICE OFFICER LINDA KNOEBEL. In 1973, Officer Linda Knoebel (pictured on the right in white Harbor Police uniform) was the first female to be hired as a San Diego Harbor Police officer who attended and completed San Diego Police Academy. She joined an existing team hired and trained for airport security duty that was formed solely as a result of the new requirements set forward by the FAA. These requirements were specifically to provide a police officer at each checkpoint and also some other specific areas within the airport all directed by the FAA. Knoebel began with the San Diego Harbor Police as the secretary to the chief of the Harbor Police (Ellsworth Kiser). As a result of her position as the chief's secretary, Knoebel was aware of the entire process that was being formed to fulfill FAA requirements for Lindbergh Field Airport. The initial group of officers was subsequently put through a short class produced by the SDPD to specifically fulfill those FAA requirements. Linda was the first Harbor Police female hired that was put through the first San Diego Police Academy where the women were fully trained to go directly on patrol in a car by themselves. There were only four women who graduated from that class—three from the San Diego Police Department and one from the San Diego Harbor Police Department, Linda Knoebel. This was a groundbreaking occurrence for the SDPD and the Harbor Police. Prior to this, all of the women graduating from the Police Academy were placed in either detective positions, school patrol, or other similar jobs. This new effort to place women on an equal basis with men was publicized as groundbreaking, as it had been a promotion-stopping problem for women, considering they could not be promoted without patrol experience. At that time, Knoebel was also the only female Harbor Police officer to attend and complete the full San Diego Navy Firefighting School located at San Diego Naval Station. Officer Knoebel and the other early female Harbor Police officers led the way with perseverance in what was then a male-dominated profession.

San Diego Municipal Employees Credit Union Annual Report 1978

HARBOR POLICE

ADVERTISEMENT FEATURING SAN DIEGO HARBOR POLICE. This advertisement from 1978 marks a new era for the Harbor Police, as it embraces the recognition of the public and other San Diego County agencies. This ad is from the San Diego Municipal Employees Credit Union, which is now the San Diego Metropolitan Credit Union. The credit union opened in 1934, as the nation was gripped by the Great Depression, to serve the employees of the City of San Diego. (Courtesy of the San Diego Unified Port District Archives.)

AIRPORT AND PATROL LINEUP. Officers posed for a photograph at the Shelter Island station in 1973. Several female officers are pictured wearing a white uniform designed for airport duty. Pictured in the first row from left to right are Officers Jay Bayman, Brian Handle, and Matthew Nastav. In the second row are Terry Bergan, Janet Chelberg, Judith Henton, Deborah Robinson-Gast, Jill Davis, Don Hadley, and Martin Hight. In the third row are John Romani, George Haines, Bob Woods, Gary Parks, Bob Moriarty, and Ray Connor. Officer Martin Hight would become chief of the Harbor Police in the 1990s, and Don Hadley became the chief of the Oceanside Police Department in the 1980s. (Courtesy of San Diego Unified Port District.)

OFFICER DEBORAH ROBINSON. One of the first women to join the Harbor Police is featured in this 1973 *San Diego Evening Tribune* article. Between 1973 and 1974, six female officers were sworn in and joined the ranks of the Harbor Police. These officers were hired to work at Lindbergh Field, providing security and traffic control. For the first three years they were on the force, female officers wore a white polyester uniform and a two-inch revolver. The first women to join the Harbor Police were Officers Judith Henton, Jill Davis, Deborah Robinson-Gast, Janet Chelberg Burgess, Linda Knoebel, Margaret Wayman, and Sherrie Pfohl. (Courtesy of the San Diego Unified Port District.)

1st women get set to foil air pirates

By JOHN FARINA
EVENING TRIBUNE *Maritime Writer*

DEBRA ROBINSON

Harbor Patrolman Debra Robinson adjusted her new police badge at Lindbergh Field yesterday, and took her first look at the passenger-screening program there designed to prevent air piracy.

Miss Robinson, 21, one of the first women to don the harbor patrolman's uniform in port district history, is undergoing an orientation program to familiarize herself with all aspects of the harbor patrolman's schedule on San Diego Bay tidelands.

But her special interest will be the airport, where at the end of the month she will take her post along with 15 other special officers, including three women, all being assigned to the task of hijack prevention.

While Miss Robinson and the other harbor patrolmen are police officers in every sense of the word, they will be specialists at the airport, trained to handle all police matters and emergencies, in addition to thwarting hijackers.

The male officers wear the regular harbor patrolmen's uniform, while the women are dressed in a uniform created especially for them.

All the officers were trained in a special six-week San Diego police academy course, and were graduated on the weekend at ceremonies on Shelter Island.

Miss Robinson was honorman, attaining the highest grade average in subjects taught, including weaponry. Her final overall score was 90.8.

Law enforcement is not a new field for Miss Robinson, because she has an associate in arts degree in criminology from Grossmont College, where she was also a member of an all-girl pistol team that brought the state championship title to the school for two years.

In addition to that, she served three years as a police intern with the San Diego Police Department in the train-

ing and traffic divisions, investigative support, and in administration planning.

"It was a solid foundation in police work," she says, "but I'll get a different view of law enforcement now because the harbor police department is a unique organization.

"It is under the San Diego Unified Port District and has responsibilities on all bay tidelands, not only the airport."

Miss Robinson will be one of five officers on duty during a shift at the airport in the federal hijack prevention program, who will be stationed at checkpoints through which all passengers boarding planes must pass.

STANDING PROUD. Three female officers stand proud, showing off their uniforms outside of Terminal 1 at Lindbergh Field. In 1973, female officers were required to wear two-inch Model 10 Smith & Wesson revolvers. (Courtesy of the San Diego Unified Port District.)

AIRPORT DUTY. Officer Sherrie Pfohl (right) stands by at Security Checkpoint No. 3, at PSA Airlines. Wackenhut Security held the contract to maintain checkpoint security in the 1970s and early 1980s, prior to the terrorist attacks of September 11, 2001. (Courtesy of the San Diego Unified Port District.)

TRAFFIC CONTROL. Harbor Police officer Stephen Clark issues a citation in front of Terminal 1 at Lindbergh Field. On April 18, 1979, a new $15-million terminal addition (now Terminal 2) was opened. (Courtesy of the San Diego Unified Port District.)

SAFETY CHECK. In 1970, a Harbor Police officer conducts a boating safety check off of Shelter Island. Harbor Police officers are required to conduct safety checks and enforce harbor and navigation codes, as well as California state boating regulations. The Harbor Police Department is the only law enforcement agency in San Diego County whose officers act as police officers as well as marine firefighters. Harbor Police Department vessels patrol San Diego Bay, its associated waterways, and coastal areas. Harbor Police vessels are staffed 24 hours a day, and in all types of weather. (Courtesy of the San Diego Unified Port District.)

HARBOR POLICE DISPATCH. Shelter Island Station was the main Harbor Police dispatch center until the early 1990s. Each officer was required to have their FCC radio operator's certification and work three-month shift rotations as a dispatcher. The Shelter Island dispatch handled both vessel and vehicle patrol dispatching, while the airport had a separate officer assigned to airport dispatch and lost and found duties. (Courtesy of the San Diego Unified Port District.)

SHELTER ISLAND STATION. Pictured here in 1977, Shelter Island Station featured a UHF/VHS radio antenna and a public pay phone. Shelter Island was constructed in 1934, and is not an actual island but, rather, is connected to the mainland by a narrow strip of land. Shelter Island was originally designated as a mud bank. The sandbar was used to dump dredgings from San Diego Bay during World War II, to allow the larger Navy ships in the bay. (Courtesy of the San Diego Unified Port District.)

HARBOR POLICE SOFTBALL TEAM. The San Diego Harbor Police softball team is pictured here in 1975. (Courtesy of Don Hadley.)

Four

THE SAN DIEGO
HARBOR POLICE
THE 1980S

The year 1980 brought the addition of a new chief of police, Arthur LeBlanc. Chief LeBlanc would bring his vast knowledge of law enforcement to the Harbor Police during the 1980s and drive the department forward. Chief LeBlanc also saw the need to expand the department's manpower and equipment.

Arthur LeBlanc enlisted in the Navy in January 1944, and served on the USS *Yellowstone*—a destroyer tender. In 1947, Arthur Leblanc began his career as a patrolman in Dearborn, Michigan. In 1959, LeBlanc moved to California and became an officer in Covina, California. In 1969, LeBlanc became the chief of police in Coronado, California, where he served until the end of 1980. He served as chief of the San Diego Harbor Police until his retirement in 1991.

CHIEF ART LEBLANC. Chief LeBlanc is remembered by his officers as a gregarious leader who loved his work. Chief LeBlanc was truly admired and loved by his officers, was known nationwide, and was widely respected among police chiefs and officers. Chief LeBlanc died on October 5, 2010, and will be forever missed by the officers of the San Diego Harbor Police. (Courtesy of the San Diego Unified Port District.)

CHRISTMAS PARTY, 1980. Arthur LeBlanc happily displays his welcoming gifts from the officers of the Harbor Police—a can of swordfish repellent and a Harbor Police chief's life ring. (Courtesy of the San Diego Unified Port District.)

OFFICER ON CAR RADIO. Pictured in 1981, this officer demonstrates the car radio in his 1980 Dodge Aspen V-8 TorqueFlite Police Pursuit Sedan. The vehicle was a four-door sedan body with a three-speed automatic power train that Dodge offered for US police use only. (Courtesy of San Diego Unified Port District.)

POLICE MOTORCYCLE. Displayed in 1981, this Harbor Police Honda motorcycle was used on Harbor Island. The motorcycle was used for traffic duties until the early 1980s. (Courtesy of San Diego Unified Port District.)

HARBOR POLICE FLEET, 1981. The Harbor Police fleet is displayed off of Shelter Island. (Courtesy of the San Diego Unified Port District.)

VESSEL EQUIPMENT DISPLAY. In the summer of 1981, officers display their fire gear on the Harbor Police dock. Officers are holding a fire entry tool and a Remington 870 police shotgun. The Remington 870 police shotgun has been in production for over 60 years and has sold over 10 million units. The Harbor Police have used the shotgun, with minor changes in its inventory, for over 50 years. (Courtesy of the San Diego Unified Port District.)

BOAT SHOW. Sgt. Robert McKnight helps host a local boat show in 1984. Sgt. McKnight is showing off Harbor Police headgear, and a small vessel. He is wearing a newly issued Smith & Wesson model 64 stainless steel revolver. The model 64 and 65 revolvers were standard issue between the early 1980s and the late 1990s. (Courtesy of the San Diego Unified Port District.)

UNIFORMS OF THE 1980S. Here, uniforms are displayed in front of the Shelter Island Police Station. From left to right are Sgt. Dave Little, displaying a standard patrol uniform consisting of dark-green, wool blend pants and a tan uniform shirt; Officer Dave Garrity, displaying the standard-issue fire gear; Officer Mark Stanger, in a green, fire retardant jumpsuit worn by vessel patrol officers. Finally, Sgt. Jen Borgen wears department dive gear. (Courtesy of the San Diego Unified Port District.)

VESSEL PATROL. Pictured here in 1989, Senior Officer Joseph Parra and Rick Holden patrol North San Diego Bay, on the vessel *Shelter Island*. The *Shelter Island* had a Livesay hull and was powered by two Mercruiser 350 engines. A third engine powered a fire pump, which could be run independently from the propulsion engines. (Courtesy of Joseph Parra.)

SHELTER ISLAND ANCHOR. In 1989, officers stand in front of the anchor at the Shelter Island Station. Placed in front of the station in the 1950s, the anchor serves as a landmark for the Harbor Police Station. While the origin of the anchor is a mystery, there were many career path discussions centered on the anchor. When officers heard "Come out to the anchor," it was time for a coaching session. Pictured from left to right are Robert Sullivan, Dominick Boccia, Dave Zacchilli, John Forsythe, Michael Elmore, and Al Bennet. (Courtesy of Dominick Boccia.)

DRUG SEIZURE, 1987. Officer Sarmiento-Markley shows off some marijuana that was seized at San Diego International Airport. (Courtesy of the San Diego Unified Port District.)

AIRFIELD SECURITY CHECKS. In 1989, Officer Jimmy Foster checks the identification of a Southwest Airlines employee while conducting a security check at Lindbergh Field. Harbor Police are responsible for law enforcement duties at the San Diego International Airport—including both the interior of the terminals and the airfield. (Courtesy of the San Diego Unified Port District.)

VIP Tour. In 1984, Officers Billy Mount and Michael Lambert took Chief LeBlanc and several officials on a tour past the Broadway Pier in San Diego Bay. In the 1980s, when boat officers saw the deck chairs coming out, they knew it was time for bay tours. Broadway Pier was constructed in 1919, and—over the years—it has accommodated passenger ships, the US Navy, and San Diego's fishing fleet. In 1983, Broadway Pier was used to host the royal yacht *Britannia*, during a visit by Queen Elizabeth. Broadway Pier was remodeled in 2010, to create a second cruise ship terminal, and can be used as a venue for public events. The Broadway Pier is located at 1000 North Harbor Drive. (Courtesy of the San Diego Unified Port District.)

Imperial Beach Pier. In the late 1980s, the pier was nearly destroyed by fire. Here, a Harbor Police vessel is fighting the pier fire. Today, the pier is the southernmost pier in California and extends 1,491 feet out into the Pacific Ocean. (Courtesy of the San Diego Unified Port District.)

EMPLOYEE APPRECIATION BREAKFAST. In 1989, Chief LeBlanc happily served (from left to right) Officer Nate Goodwin and administrative assistants Phyllis Carpenter and Carmelita Hawkins at the employee appreciation breakfast. Every year, the employees of the San Diego Unified Port District were rewarded for their service at this breakfast. (Courtesy of the San Diego Unified Port District.)

HARBOR POLICE DIVE TEAM. These officers are pictured in 1989 in front of the Shelter Island Station. From left to right, the divers are Richard Skoryi, Rick Holden, Fred Curtis, Robert Mickschl, Mark Nail, Rick Castle, Steven Bodamer, Robert McKnight, and Rick Robershaw. (Courtesy of Brad Hizer.)

AIR FORCE ONE. In this 1988 photograph, Sgt. Ken Franke stands in front of *Air Force One*. Sgt. Franke supervised Harbor Police officers during Pres. Ronald Reagan's visit to Lindbergh Field. (Courtesy of Ken Franke.)

ROLE-PLAY. In this photograph from 1989, Harbor Police recruits Dave King and Doug Welker hold the perimeter during a mock bank robbery. Recruit King is communicating on a handheld radio, and Recruit Welker holds a Smith & Wesson revolver. This was the last academy class in San Diego County to be taught the revolver exclusively. Later academy classes transitioned to training with semiautomatic handguns. Recruits are required to undergo training scenarios, such as this one, to prepare them for the field. (Courtesy of Dave King.)

THE THINKER. Recruit Dave King is seen deep in concentration during a criminal law class at the San Diego Sheriff's Academy in 1989. (Courtesy of Dave King.)

Five

THE SAN DIEGO HARBOR POLICE
THE 1990S

The 1990s brought tremendous change to the San Diego Harbor Police. The city of San Diego was growing, and the Harbor Police had to keep up. The 1990s were spent preparing the department for the 21st century, and the new chief of the Harbor Police would find it necessary for the department to take on additional roles and nearly double in size. The department was maturing and becoming a full-service police agency, necessitating its move to a new location. The decade also saw the addition of an investigative unit and a Harbor Police Explosive Detection K-9 team, and the assignment of officers to the San Diego International Airport Narcotics Task Force and the US Customs Marine Task Force.

HARBOR POLICE CHIEF MARTIN HIGHT. Chief Hight served as chief of police from October 1991 to July 1999. Chief Hight started as a Harbor Police officer and worked his way up the ranks—becoming a sergeant in 1978, and captain in 1985. In his years of service to the Harbor Police, Hight saw the department grow from a force of about 60 officers to the current force of 115 officers that was established in 1999. (Courtesy of the San Diego Unified Port District Archives.)

HARBOR POLICE HEADQUARTERS. The early 1990s saw the renovation of the above San Diego Harbor Police facility, located at 3380 North Harbor Drive. Built in 1948, the building was the home of the Lockheed Corporation's offices. Now the headquarters for the Harbor Police, the new building houses the police administration and patrol functions of the department. (Courtesy of the San Diego Unified Port District.)

1990 GROUP PICTURE. Officers group together on the Harbor Police vessel in this photograph. Pictured clockwise from left are Officers Donald Brick, Robert Sullivan, Richard Skoryi, Joseph Sharp, John Drake, and an unidentified California Fish and Game officer, and Brian Jensen. (Courtesy of Harbor Police Sergeant Brian Jensen.)

DISPATCH DUTIES. Officer Jeffrey Abbey works the dispatch desk at Shelter Island in this 1994 photograph. Officer Abbey passed away on November 17, 2004, following a tragic accident. Officer Abbey worked with the force for 17 years and was known as a dedicated law enforcer, whose compassion for his coworkers and his community was nothing short of exemplary. Several years later (after the death of Jeffrey Abbey), the Harbor Police opened a new dispatch center that was staffed by professional dispatchers, thus relieving officers for patrol duties. (Courtesy of the San Diego Unified Port District.)

TRAFFIC STOP. Officer Terry Anderson writes a motorist a citation on North Harbor Drive in this photograph from the early 1990s. The Holiday Inn, located at 1355 North Harbor Drive, can be seen in the background. It is now a Wyndham hotel. (Courtesy of the San Diego Unified Port District.)

JET SKI TEAM. Here, Officers Chris Moore and Donald Brick patrol South San Diego Bay on jet skis. In the 1990s, the San Diego Unified Port District initiated a program utilizing jet skis in the shallow South San Diego Bay waters. The jet skis were used in environmentally sensitive areas to enforce boating speed laws while preserving endangered species. (Courtesy of the San Diego Unified Port District.)

IMPERIAL BEACH SANDCASTLE COMPETITION. Officers David Garrity and Sal Colin are pictured here wearing the new LAPD-style dark-blue uniforms. The officers were providing security at a sandcastle-building competition. The competition originated in 1981, when a group of Imperial Beach residents formed the first Sandcastle Days Committee. The event's proceeds went to benefit the Boys & Girls Clubs of America. The sandcastle competition had its last year at Imperial Beach in 2011. The Imperial Beach Pier and adjacent park area is maintained by the San Diego Unified Port District. The Imperial Beach Pier was constructed in 1909 to house the Edwards Wave Motor—a piece of machinery that generated electricity using the tides. (Courtesy of the San Diego Unified Port District.)

HARBOR POLICE BIKE TEAM. In the late 1990s, the Harbor Police introduced a bike team to reach out to the community and police the waterfront. Here, Officers Doug Welker and Bill Kellerman patrol the area adjacent to Seaport Village Shopping Center. (Courtesy of the San Diego Unified Port District.)

CHIEF DAVE HALL. Sworn in as the Harbor Police chief on July 19, 1999, Dave Hall began his career as a police officer with the San Diego Police Department and retired, with the rank of captain, after 30 years of service. (Courtesy of the San Diego Unified Port District.)

FIRE EQUIPMENT DEMONSTRATION. Pictured here in 1996, Sgt. Robert Mickschl demonstrates fire equipment to a student aboard a Harbor Police vessel. The student is holding a fire line and nozzle that is used off of the vessel's rear fire monitor. (Courtesy of the San Diego Unified Port District.)

COMMAND VAN. In the 1990s, the Harbor Police recognized that times were changing and that they would need to take a leadership role in preparing the tidelands and airport for major incidents. Pictured here is the first of two Harbor Police command vehicles. The command van featured mobile radio and lighting systems, designed for command and control during major events. (Courtesy of the San Diego Unified Port District.)

Six

THE MAKING OF A 21ST CENTURY DEPARTMENT
A NEW PARADIGM FOR POLICING

As they entered the 21st century, the San Diego Harbor Police were forced to face the terrorist attacks of September 11, 2001, and two wildfires in San Diego County—the Cedar Fire of October 2003, and the Witch Creek Fire of October 2007.

On September 11, 2001, a series of four coordinated terrorist attacks—perpetrated by the al-Qaeda terrorist group—were launched against New York City and the Washington, DC, metropolitan area. The attacks occurred while it was still the early morning in San Diego, and operations at San Diego International Airport were running as normal. At approximately 5:46 a.m., Pacific Time, Flight 11 crashed into the north face of the World Trade Center's North Tower at approximately 466 miles per hour. As faces were glued to TV screens, Harbor Police officers moved into action—mobilizing all units and coordinating a mandatory call out of all off-duty officers.

Two years later, on October 25, 2003, San Diego was tested by the largest wildfire in California's history. The Cedar Fire started 25 miles east of San Diego, in the Cleveland National Forest. By October 26, 2003, the Cedar Fire crossed into San Diego County and every county law enforcement agency sprang into action. The San Diego Harbor Police again conducted a call out of off duty officers and formed Mobile Field Force squads to assist with traffic control, evacuations, and theft prevention in the affected areas of the county.

In all, over 50 engine companies were used against the fires. By October 28, the Cedar Fire had destroyed 280,278 acres of land and 2,820 buildings. Fifteen people were killed.

On October 20, 2007, California was struck again by wildfires—causing the Harbor Police to jump to the assistance of the greater San Diego County. The 2007 wildfires burned 500,000 acres, destroyed 1,500 homes, and caused nine deaths. The San Diego Harbor Police provided 24-hour mutual aid squads, headed up by Lt. Ken Franke. Officers provided evacuation assistance, security, and traffic direction, all while enduring extreme heat and Santa Ana winds that reached 85 miles per hour.

Additionally, the Harbor Police formed a senior volunteer program, a chaplain program, and would soon see the addition of a new fleet of fire and patrol vessels. In response to the terrorist attacks of September 11th, the Harbor Police also formed a Maritime Tactical Response Team and issued all of its officers with tactical rifles for daily patrol use.

HARBOR POLICE TACTICAL RIFLE. Pictured here in 2004, Sgt. Brian Jensen demonstrates the deployment of his Colt M4 Carbine from the patrol vehicle. Harbor Police was the first agency in San Diego County to issue all officers a rifle for daily use in patrol. (Courtesy of the San Diego Unified Port District.)

Chief Betty P. Kelepecz. In August 2003, the Harbor Police welcomed Chief Betty Kelepecz—the first female chief of the Harbor Police. Chief Kelepecz had worked her way up the ranks of the LAPD, from 1980 to 2003, and had previously attained the rank of commander. Chief Kelepecz is considered a pioneer in the area of women attaining police command positions. (Courtesy of the San Diego Unified Port District.)

PRES. GEORGE W. BUSH. Seen here during his 2001 visit, Pres. Bush (center) poses with Harbor Police Explosive K-9 unit members Michael Rich, Barry Snell, and Marc Brakebill; and airport officers Sal Colin, Don Claypool, and Jim Rymut. In 1996, the Harbor Police Explosive Detection was formed with two K-9 teams. Currently, the Harbor Police has six K-9 explosives teams, who are responsible for explosives detection at San Diego International Airport and are on call throughout San Diego County. (Courtesy of Michael Rich.)

PRES. JIMMY CARTER. In 2002, Cpl. Dominick Boccia and his K-9, Yurrie, took a moment to pose with Pres. Jimmy Carter at San Diego International Airport. (Courtesy of Lt. Dominick Boccia.)

HARBOR POLICE NEWSLETTER CARTOON. In 2003, Officer Paul Garcia drew this good-humored cartoon for the Harbor Police department newsletter. Officer Garcia is depicting the fire-training trailer, where officers were required to climb through a pitch-black maze consisting of multiple layers and turns. The training trailer was designed teach officers about the hazards of working a fire with limited to no visibility. (Courtesy of Connie Thomas and Paul Garcia.)

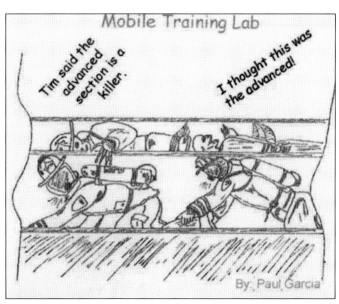

EXHAUSTED OFFICER. Firefighting training has seemingly taken a toll on this officer, as he recovers after exiting a burning structure. Harbor Police officers are required to attend a two-week marine firefighting course after joining the department, as well as undergo a separate vessel crewman certification class. (Courtesy of David Marshall.)

FIRE EQUIPMENT. Cpl. Victor Banuelos carries a one-and-three-fourths-inch fire hose following a vessel fire on Harbor Island. Officers are required to be proficient in the handling of fire equipment. (Photograph by Arash Afshar, courtesy of the San Diego Unified Port District.)

LONG DAY OF FIRE TRAINING. Harbor Police fire instructors poses for a photograph after training on a Harbor Police burn boat. These vessels are used for actual firefighting, so that officers can become comfortable with onboard firefighting. Pictured in the first row are (from left to right) Officers Greg Avalos, Jeff Geary, and Robert Adauto. In the second row are Officers Shawn Wooddy, Christopher Scheil, and Sean Culhane, and Sgt. Donald Brick, (Courtesy of the San Diego Unified Port District.)

FIRE TRAINING. Officers suppress a fire in the interior of a vessel in this photograph. The San Diego Harbor Police holds periodic fire training courses for all of its officers, and all officers are required to demonstrate proficiency in both firefighting and the wearing of protective gear. (Courtesy of the San Diego Unified Port District.)

VESSEL FIRE. Officers attempt to extinguish a blazing vessel fire on Harbor Island in 2013. The officers in this photograph are docked several vessels downwind of the fire, in the new FireStorm vessel. They are laying a one-and-three-fourths-inch line to the fire. After the fire is suppressed, officers will enter the vessel in search of further hazards. (Courtesy of the San Diego Unified Port District.)

NEW TECHNOLOGY. Officer Robert Adauto's cartoon from the Harbor Police newsletter pokes fun at the department's grasping of new technology. The early 2000s brought mobile computers, license plate readers, and cameras to department vehicles, enabling officers to work more independently in the field. (Courtesy of Connie Thomas and Robert Adauto.)

"I know we're trying to save money here, but these new radios are ridiculous!"

VEHICLE TECHNOLOGY. Officer Roberto Padilla runs a vehicle's license plate on his cruiser's computer. The vehicle's dashboard camera system is also visible. (Photograph by Arash Afshar, San Diego Unified Port District Archives.)

PADRES LAW ENFORCEMENT NIGHT. Sgt. Charles Marks tips his hat to the crowd as he appears on the JumboTron at PETCO Park. This event recognizes the members of the law enforcement community, and a pre-game ceremony highlights more than 50 local, state, and federal law enforcement agencies. A portion of the proceeds from these games goes toward law enforcement charities. (Courtesy of the San Diego Unified Port District Archives.)

Chief Kirk Sanfilippo. Kirk Sanfilippo joined the San Diego Harbor Police force in October 2003 and served as captain until April 7, 2005, when he was sworn in as chief of the Harbor Police. He previously served 22 years with the Sunnyvale Department of Public Safety. (Courtesy of the San Diego Unified Port District.)

SENIOR VOLUNTEERS. Since the early 2000s, the Harbor Police has welcomed senior volunteers to the department. Senior volunteers assist the department with traffic control and vessel security patrols, issue parking citations, and conduct marina security checks. Here, senior volunteers Joni Strong (left) and Henri Kuhn stop for a photograph while on patrol. (Courtesy of the San Diego Unified Port District Archives.)

HONOR GUARD. Retired sergeant Robert McKnight plays "Amazing Grace" on the bagpipes while representing the San Diego Harbor Police Honor Guard at a funeral. Sgt. McKnight served for over 20 years with the Harbor Police and supervised the Harbor Police Dive Team. (Courtesy of the San Diego Unified Port District.)

HONOR GUARD. In this photograph, the Harbor Police Honor Guard stands proud during a pre-game at a San Diego Padres game at PETCO Park. This group represents the department at many San Diego County events. Pictured from left to right are Robert McKnight, Gregory Scallion, Laura Sweeney, Jennifer Spearel, and James Jordan. (Courtesy of the San Diego Unified Port District.)

MINOR ACCIDENTS HAPPEN.
This 2003 newsletter
cartoon by Officer Paul
Garcia makes light of a
minor boating accident.
(Courtesy of Connie
Thomas and Paul Garcia.)

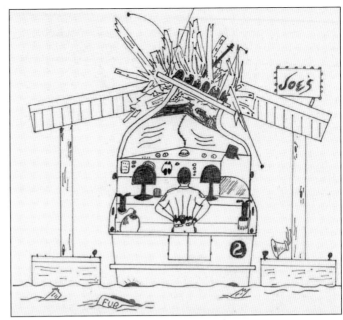

METALCRAFT FIRESTORM 36. In January 2004, the Environmental Protection Agency mandated new emission regulations for any new commercial marine diesel engines installed on vessels flagged or registered in the United States. In 2009, the Harbor Police were awarded a grant from the Department of Homeland Security to assist with the purchase of new vessels. The FireStorm 36, which had a new Cummins QSB 5.9 engine, was chosen as it was cleaner starting, produced less noise, and virtually eliminated the smoke and odor traditionally associated with diesel engines. These new motors were not only lighter and more fuel-efficient, they significantly enhanced the department's response time. The vessels were enhanced with Hamilton jets, which made the vessels much more maneuverable and made it easier to respond to rescue calls in shallow waters. The vessels are capable of reaching speeds of approximately 38 knots. Each vessel is equipped with three fire monitors and is capable of pumping 2,500 gallons of water per minute. (Courtesy of the San Diego Unified Port District.)

14TH DALAI LAMA. Cpl. Damith Rodrigo (right) was able to meet His Holiness, the 14th Dalai Lama (left), on April 20, 2012, and received an extremely rare opportunity to chant a Buddhist blessing with him. The Dalai Lama was in San Diego on his first official visit for the "Compassion Without Borders" conference. On his trip to San Diego, the Dalai Lama entrusted his protection

to officers from the San Diego Harbor Police. Cpl. Rodrigo grew up in Sri Lanka and came to the United States at age 17, and he is the only Buddhist police officer of Sri Lankan descent in San Diego County. (Courtesy of the San Diego Unified Port District.)

WEAPONS TRAINING UNIT. Team members pose with their tactical gear after a long day of training at the Escondido Police Range. These officers are showing off the wide array of weapons at their disposal, including a Colt M4 Model R0977 equipped with a suppressor. The team—led by Sgts. Boccia and Jenson—are, from left to right, (first row) Jarred Osselaer, Brian Jensen, Dominick Boccia, and Bob Twardy; (second row) Sam Davis, Mike Dye, Pedro Acre, Mike Bishop, Eric Mitchell, Troy Nicol, Joe "Booger" Sharp, and Chris Moore. (Courtesy of Lt. Dominick Boccia.)

SOCCER MATCH. On September 22, 2012, the Harbor Police departmental soccer team hosted an international match against the Household Cavalry football team. The British team had just arrived from the United Kingdom and was starting its 2012 football tour on the West Coast. The Harbor Police players were joined by players from the San Diego County Sheriff's Office. The "real" harbor team members were Assistant Chief Mark Stainbrook, Lt. Dominick Boccia, and Officers Raul Munoz, Ryan Eldred, Aldo Gutierrez, Daniel Moen, Eric Willms, and Andres Mendoza. The San Diego Sheriff's Office players were Felipe Cabral, Tyler Norby, Victor Lemos, Mike Bravo, Eduardo Banuelos, Carlos Rueda, and Jorge Gonzales. The Household Cavalry Mounted Regiment is a ceremonial cavalry regiment of the British Army. It is classed as a regiment of guards, and carries out ceremonial duties on state and royal occasions. (Courtesy of Lt. Dominick Boccia,)

OCTOBER 20, 2007, CALIFORNIA WILDFIRE. Smoke rises in the area of Jamul California. During the fires, Harbor Police officers manned checkpoints and assisted with round-the-clock evacuations alongside other San Diego County police agencies. (Courtesy of Michael P. Rich.)

SMOKE OVER SAN DIEGO BAY. In October 2007, smoke enveloped most of San Diego—including the San Diego Bay. Here, a cruise ship departs the bay through the smoke. The fires of 2007 left behind a thick layer of ash and smoke that spread as far as Northern California. (Courtesy of Ken Franke.)

2007 WILDFIRE GROUP PHOTO. San Diego County agencies worked together during the fire and were divided up in platoons, each supervised by a lieutenant. Pictured here are officers from the San Diego County Sheriff, Immigration and Customs Enforcement, Harbor Police, and the California Department of Justice. (Courtesy of the San Diego Unified Port District.)

BAKER TO VEGAS. In this 2000 photograph, officers man a rescue vehicle for the annual Baker to Vegas race. Every year, the Harbor Police Department participates in the Baker to Vegas Relay—a 120-mile relay race from Baker, California, to Las Vegas, Nevada. About 10,000 law enforcement officers from across the world participate in the April event, which makes it the largest running law enforcement event in the world. (Courtesy Salvador Colon.)

ARNOLD SCHWARZENEGGER VISITS. Harbor Police sergeant Brian Jensen escorts Arnold Schwarzenegger for a visit to the Sector Command of the US Coast Guard in San Diego on October 12, 2006. It is rumored that Sergeant Jensen gave bodybuilding tips to Governor Schwarzenegger. The Austrian-born actor, film producer, and former professional bodybuilder, served as the governor of California from 2003 to 2011. (Courtesy of the San Diego Unified Port District.)

RED BULL AIR RACE. This photograph, taken by Officer Dave Marshall, shows a moment from a Red Bull air race, as one of the planes slices through an inflatable event barricade. The 2010 Red Bull World Series took place over San Diego Bay, between Coronado and the parks of the Embarcadero Marina. (Courtesy of Dave Marshall.)

RED BULL AIR RACE. In this photograph, a plane takes a side turn during the air race and passes in front of the Hyatt Hotel in San Diego. (Courtesy of Dave Marshall.)

HARBOR POLICE DIVE TEAM. Dive team members Dave Marshall, Jeff Geary, Steve Bailey, Dell Macgray, and Greg Avalos conduct dive training in San Diego Bay in the winter of 2009. The officers are using a 32-foot SAFE Boat, which has twin Mercury 250 outboard engines. The SAFE Boat reaches a top speed of between 40 and 45 miles per hour. (Courtesy of the San Diego Unified Port District.)

DIVE TEAM TRAINING. Officer Ramon Colon takes part in underwater dive training in this photograph. The Harbor Police dive team conducts monthly dive training, including underwater searches, rescue operations, and underwater explosive ordnance detection. The Harbor Police dive team consists of 20 members and is supervised by two sergeants. (Courtesy of Ramon Colon.)

Suiting Up. Cpl. Victor Banuelos prepares for a dive in San Diego Bay—donning a dry suit that includes a full-face mask and communications equipment. (Courtesy of the San Diego Unified Port District.)

BIOTECH, DECEMBER 2001. Officers of the San Diego Harbor Police took a group photo while working at a biotech convention in San Diego. Expecting a massive protest, local agencies formed mutual aid platoons. Due to the overwhelming police presence, any violent protests were averted. The convention attracted 14,000 attendees and was an outstanding success. The anti-biotechnology protesters had a variety of grievances and staged a loud, colorful, and peaceful demonstration. (Courtesy of the San Diego Unified Port District.)

OCCUPY SAN DIEGO. On December 10, 2011, San Diego Harbor Police and the San Diego Police Department provided security for the Occupy San Diego protests. Occupy San Diego's intention was to blockade shipping operations at the marine terminal. Four protesters were eventually arrested for criminal behavior. The San Diego protesters occupied the San Diego Civic Center for several weeks as well as staging several day protests at the San Diego Harbor. (Courtesy of the San Diego Unified Port District.)

MARITIME TACTICAL TRAINING. Officers Bankhead, Bailey, and Hart practice the tactical boarding of vessels on San Diego Bay. The San Diego Harbor Police are trained for high-risk boardings of both commercial and private vessels, in the event of a hostage situation or terrorist incident. (Courtesy of the San Diego Unified Port District.)

CHIEF JOHN BOLDUC. On May 14, 2010, John Bolduc was sworn in as the new chief of the Harbor Police. Previously the chief of police in Brainerd, Minnesota, Bolduc came to the Harbor Police with more than 23 years of experience in municipal policing, specializing in tactical teams, training, and leadership development. He was involved in the professional training and development of police chiefs and supervisors throughout Minnesota. (Courtesy of San Diego Unified Port District.)

MILITARY SERVICE. In this 2009 photograph, Officer Jim Rymut is welcomed back from military service in Afghanistan. James Rymut was a first sergeant in the US Army Special Forces with over 30 years of service—including service in Vietnam. The Harbor Police has always honored its military reservists for their service to their country. (Courtesy of Joe Sharp.)

FLAG OF THE UNITED STATES OF AMERICA. This flag was flown above the combined joint special operations task force compound at Bagram Airfield, Afghanistan, on December 26, 2003, during Operation Enduring Freedom. The flag was flown in honor of the San Diego Harbor Police and was presented to the Harbor Police by Command Sgt. Maj. George Bequer and Officer James Rymut. (Courtesy of Michael P. Rich.)

VEHICLE STOP TRAINING. Officer Jennifer Spearel conducts a traffic stop on Officer Paul Garcia, who is driving his 2004 Lamborghini Gallardo. (Courtesy of the San Diego Unified Port District.)

CHILDREN'S CANCER SURVIVOR EVENT. Officer Troy Nicol volunteers at an event to raise money and awareness for cancer survival. (Courtesy of the San Diego Unified Port District.)

SHOP WITH A COP. Chief John Bolduc rides with a child during the annual Shop with a Cop event in 2012. The event benefits needy or neglected children from across San Diego County. Shop with a Cop takes place every December and provides a memorable shopping experience for underprivileged children. The children are chosen by schools, churches, and social services agencies. Uniformed officers from local, state, and federal agencies volunteer their time to be with the children, and each child is provided with a $100 Target gift card to spend on themselves and their family. (Courtesy of Salvador Colin.)

BIKE TEAM. In this 2006 photograph, officers working the Harbor Police bike team stop in front of the G Street Pier area for a rest. Officers that work the bike patrol find that mobility is the primary benefit to riding a bike versus working in a patrol car. The Harbor Police bike team has built trust with both port tenants and the visiting public. Pictured from left to right are Joseph Parra, Laura Tosatto, Tony Hazzard, and Pete Quiroz. (Courtesy of Joseph Parra.)

TRAFFIC TEAM. Officer Kenneth Helman writes a bicyclist a citation on North Harbor Drive. The Harbor Police traffic team's mission is to lower the rate of traffic accidents and ensure a safe area for public travel. (Courtesy of Kenneth Helman.)

Seven

THE SAN DIEGO HARBOR POLICE

THE UNIFORMS AND EQUIPMENT OF THE HARBOR POLICE

As the Harbor Police formed a new department from a quiet security force in the 1950s, the officers began to recognize their own elite department within the county of San Diego. Law enforcement officers in the early 1950s wore thick wool pants and wool blend shirts. Upon the forming of the Port of San Diego Harbor Police, the departments chose the style of the San Diego County Sheriff Department, consisting of dark green pants and a tan shirt. The uniform remained unchanged except for the patch change until the early 1980s when the department adopted a dark green cotton jumpsuit for vessel patrol use. In the late 1980s, officers were given the option of shorts for vessel and bike patrol use. Uniforms were beginning to become more user-friendly for the environmental changes and for fire safety.

UNIFORMS OF THE HARBOR POLICE. Pictured in 2007, these officers are displaying the different uniform variations for special assignment and patrol. Pictured in on the dock are (from left to right) the mutual aid tactical uniform, the bike team uniform, and the dress patrol uniform. Pictured on the boat are (from left to right) the honor guard uniforms, the K-9 team uniform, the boat crewperson uniform, the weapons training uniform, the retired senior volunteer uniforms, the dive team uniform, and the firefighting uniform. (Courtesy of the San Diego Unified Port District.)

FIRST FEMALE UNIFORM VARIATION. This white polyester uniform was in use from 1973 to 1975. For the first two years, female officers on the Harbor Police wore a two-inch Smith & Wesson sidearm. Pictured is Officer Judy Henton. (Courtesy of the San Diego Unified Port District.)

SECOND VARIATION FEMALE UNIFORM. This tan and green uniform became the standard-issue uniform worn by female officers from 1975 to the early 1990s. The green and tan uniforms were also standard issue among male officers from 1957 to the early 1990s. Pictured is Officer Sherrie Pfohl. (Courtesy of the San Diego Unified Port District.)

EARLY-ISSUE DRESS HAT. Pictured here is an eight-point hat from the 1950s. This style of hat was first worn by the NYPD in 1928. This hat has a gold band and simple "P" screw post, to fasten the band to the hat. The hat features the gold first-issue hat badge, bearing the words "Harbor Police." Officers were required to wear the hat while on vessel and vehicle patrols. This style of hat was worn by the Harbor Police from the early 1950s, until the late 1960s. The badge on this early hat was manufactured by V.H. Blackinton & Co., Inc., of Attleboro Falls, Massachusetts. Blackinton has been in business since 1852. (Courtesy of Michael P. Rich.)

LATE-ISSUE DRESS HAT. This dress hat was worn by Harbor Police in the 1990s. This style of hat entered into service with the Harbor Police in the late 1960s and remained in use as a standard uniform item until the early 1980s. Currently, this style of dress hat is worn only by the Harbor Police Honor Guard. The badge pictured on this dress hat is the second-issue hat badge produced by the C.W. Nielson MFG Corporation of Chehalis, Washington. (Courtesy of Michael P. Rich.)

CHIEF'S BALL CAP. Art LeBlanc wore this ball cap during his tenure as chief of police in the early 1980s. The leaf-shaped embellishments on the cap's visor, commonly called "scrambled eggs," are gold embroidery. This is reserved for command staff level officers, and is usually seen in military—and some civilian—use. This green, nylon ball cap was also the standard-issue cap worn by Harbor Police officers on vessel patrol, from the 1980s to the 1990s. Officers were not allowed to wear ball caps while working at the airport or during vehicle patrol assignments. (Courtesy of Lt. Dominick Boccia.)

DUTY HELMET. The plastic duty helmet was standard issue for the Harbor Police from 1961 until the late 1990s. Officers were issued a detachable plastic face shield for crowd control and were required to have the helmets at hand during their shifts. This style of helmet was eventually replaced by a heavier, standard-issue ballistic helmet. (Courtesy of Michael P. Rich.)

HARBOR DEPARTMENT LANTERN. This photograph is of a vintage c. 1910 City of San Diego Harbor Department lantern. The lantern is a Handlan-brand lantern with "Property of City of San Diego Harbor Department." This lantern was used at the intersection of Broadway and North Harbor Drive between 1910 and 1946. (Courtesy of Michael P. Rich.)

STANDARD-ISSUE FIRE HELMET. This is the Harbor Police's standard-issue fire helmet. The helmet, which is made of Kevlar, is equipped with a mounted flashlight and goggles. This helmet was worn by a Harbor Police officer in a fire and has been damaged by intense heat. Protective fire gear is required to be carried by Harbor Police officers while on vessel and vehicle patrol. (Courtesy of David Marshall.)

FIRST-ISSUE PATCH. This Harbor Police shoulder patch was worn from 1957 to 1964. This patch was fully embroidered and featured the City of San Diego seal in the center of a white flag. The flag patch was worn on the left shoulder of the uniform shirt and jacket. The official seal of the City of San Diego was adopted by the city on April 14, 1914. It features the Pillars of Hercules, and the winged wheel represents manufacturing and transportation. The two connected dolphins symbolize the Pacific and Atlantic Oceans—united by the Panama Canal—and the motto, "Semper Vigilans," means "ever vigilant." The seal also features an orange, which represents agriculture, and a Spanish caravel representing exploration and settlement by the Spanish. Finally, the wavy blue band below the seal represents the city's position on the sea. (Courtesy of Lt. Dominick Boccia.)

SECOND-ISSUE PATCH. This Harbor Police shoulder patch was worn on officers' left shoulders from 1964 to 1969. The fully embroidered patch featured the Port of San Diego emblem in the center of a white flag. The Port of San Diego seal depicts the Cabrillo National Monument on Point Loma. The monument is located at the southern tip of the Point Loma Peninsula, in San Diego. The monument commemorates the landing of Juan Rodríguez Cabrillo at San Diego Bay, on September 28, 1542. (Courtesy of Lt. Dominick Boccia.)

HARBOR POLICE PATCHES. Pictured here are a number of San Diego Harbor Police patches, issued between 1969 and the present. From left to right, on the top row, is the third-issue uniform shoulder patch (1969–1980); the fourth-issue shoulder patch (1980 to present), with the Senior Volunteer rocker above it, the traffic officer patch, and the community services officer patch. In the second row is a jacket badge patch (1987–1995), a weapons training unit patch, a first aid patch (1957–1965), a vessel accident investigator patch, a cap patch (1985–1999), a jacket patch (1995–2005), a dive team patch (1985–1995), and a cap flag patch (1980–1985). On the bottom are a number of jacket badge patches and life jacket badge patches (2005–present). (Courtesy of Michael P. Rich.)

HARBOR DEPARTMENT BADGE.
Pictured here is a c. 1948 San Diego
Harbor Department badge. This is
a metal badge that was issued to the
chief of the Harbor Department. In
1948, the department consisted of a
chief and five patrolmen. Members
of the Harbor Department were
City of San Diego employees.
(Courtesy of Michael P. Rich.)

SAN DIEGO HARBOR POLICE BADGE.
Pictured here is a pre-1962 San Diego
Harbor Police nickel-plated badge. This
badge was issued to an officer between
1950 and 1962. It features the official
seal of the City of San Diego, outlined
by a white enamel ring and blue enamel
lettering. (Courtesy of Michael P. Rich.)

113

SAN DIEGO HARBOR POLICE PATROLMAN BADGE. Pictured here is a patrolman's badge that was issued between 1963 and 1970. This badge is a gold-tone metal badge with a white enamel circle around the Port of San Diego's official seal. This was the first badge issued to the San Diego Unified Port District Harbor Police. The badge was manufactured by the Entenmann-Rovin Company, in Los Angeles. The Entenmann-Rovin badge company introduced their "Carltone" gold finish, which was formulated to produce a glossy finish. (Courtesy of Michael P. Rich.)

POLICE OFFICER BADGE. Pictured here is a San Diego Harbor Police officer's badge. This badge was issued between 1970 and 1980. These badges were issued when the title "police officer" replaced that of "patrolman." This badge was the second pattern issued to the San Diego Unified Port District Harbor Police. (Courtesy of Michael P. Rich.)

SENIOR POLICE OFFICER. Pictured is the badge of a senior police officer, which was in service from 1980 through the 1990s. This badge was manufactured by the Sun Badge Company. The Sun Badge Company is based in Ontario, California, and has been in business for over 45 years. The rank of senior officer was later changed to that of corporal, which is still an official rank in the Harbor Police. (Courtesy of Michael P. Rich.)

CURRENT-ISSUE BADGE. The current badge features the Point Loma Lighthouse, with the San Diego Unified Port District seal in its center. The Point Loma Lighthouse is located on the Point Loma peninsula, at the mouth of San Diego Bay. The lighthouse is no longer in operation but is open as a museum. This authorized badge is produced by the Sun Badge Company, of Ontario, California. (Courtesy of Michael P. Rich.)

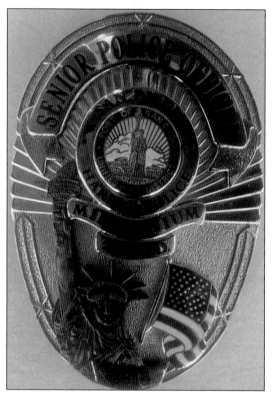

MILLENNIUM BADGE. This was an optional badge that was worn from 2000 to 2001 to celebrate the new millennium. The badge features the Statue of Liberty and the American flag below the San Diego Unified Port District seal. This authorized badge was produced in 2001 by V&V Manufacturing, of City of Industry, California. (Courtesy of Michael P. Rich.)

UNITED 9/11 BADGE. This was an optional badge that was authorized for wear by police officers and firefighters in San Diego County during the month of September 2011, marking the 10th anniversary of the terrorist attacks of September 11, 2001. The badge features the World Trade Center's Twin Towers, with the number 343 on one and the number 60 on the other—representing the number of firefighters and police officers who lost their lives in the attacks. The numbers appear under the word "united," which is spelled out in red, white, and blue, and the Port District seal is located in the center of the Pentagon. This authorized badge was produced by the Entenmann-Rovin Co., of Los Angeles. (Courtesy of Michael P. Rich.)

50TH ANNIVERSARY BADGE. This is the San Diego Harbor Police's 50th anniversary badge. This was an optional badge that was worn in 2012. The badge depicts a jet in the upper center—representing San Diego International Airport—and two vessels that represent the marine duties of the Harbor Police. The seal of the Port of San Diego and an anchor finish off the badge. The badge was manufactured by Collinson Enterprises in 2011, and served as a limited edition authorized badge for the San Diego Harbor Police. (Courtesy of Michael P. Rich.)

AMERICA'S FIRST RESPONDERS UNITED BADGE. This optional badge was introduced in 2012 and can be worn during the month of September. The badge is worn nationwide by police, fire, and federally recognized EMS first responders. The idea is that all first responders wear the same badge because they share the same mission. This authorized badge was manufactured by Absolute Victory Insignia because, according to their website, "Should another attack occur, we'll respond because we're united in the business of saving lives. Even if it means risking our own lives to do so." (Courtesy of Michael P. Rich.)

PORT DISTRICT COMMISSIONER. These badges were issued to San Diego Unified Port District commissioners in the early 1980s. Commissioner badges were gifted to Port District commissioners by Chief Art LeBlanc, upon their being sworn in to the Board of Port Commissioners. The badge pictured was manufactured by V.H. Blackinton & Co., Inc., of Attleboro Falls, Massachusetts—which has been in business since 1852. The badge has blue enamel lettering and a white enamel ring surrounding the Port District seal. The port is governed by a seven-member Board of Port Commissioners, with one commissioner each appointed by the city councils of Coronado, Chula Vista, Imperial Beach, and National City, and three appointed by San Diego. (Courtesy of Michael P. Rich.)

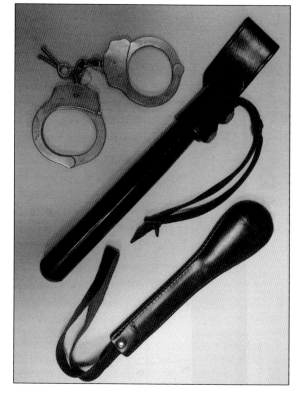

BILLY CLUB. Pictured are several items carried by Officer William Hall in the 1950s. From left to right are a pair of Peerless brand handcuffs, a wooden baton, and a leather sap. A sap is a flat impact weapon, shaped like a beaver tail and weighted with lead on at least one end. Saps are no longer carried by the Harbor Police. (Courtesy of Todd Jarvis.)

Model 10, Two Inch. This revolver was carried by female Harbor Police officers, from 1973 to 1975. It is a two-inch Smith & Wesson model 10. (Courtesy of Michael P. Rich.)

Model 10, Four Inch. This weapon was carried by Harbor Police officers, from 1956 until the early 1980s. It is a four-inch Smith & Wesson model 10. (Courtesy of Michael P. Rich.)

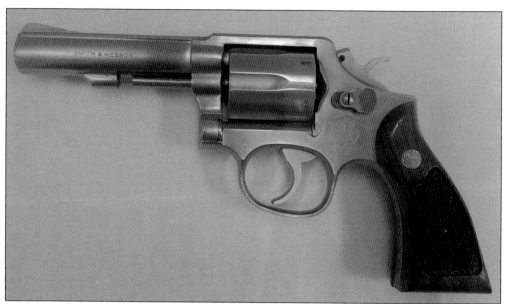

MODEL 64 SMITH & WESSON. This .38 caliber Smith & Wesson revolver was carried by Harbor Police officers, from the early 1980s until the late 1990s. The revolver was eventually replaced as a police sidearm by 9 mm. and .40 caliber Glock semiautomatic handguns. (Courtesy of Lt. Dominick Boccia.)

GLOCK 23. Since the late 1990s, the Harbor Police has issued its officers with Glock semiautomatic handguns. Pictured is the .40 caliber Glock model 23, in the Gen 4 series. Glock has become one of the most common makes of sidearm carried by law enforcement and military personnel, featuring high-tech, polymer gun frame construction. (Courtesy of Michael P. Rich.)

Eight

THE HARBOR POLICE
A FAMILY UNITED

In March 2014, the Harbor Police Department was surprised by a visit from Oregon state trooper John Riddle—the grandson of Harbor Police officer John C. Riddle. John C. Riddle was one of the first San Diego Harbor Police officers hired under Chief Kiser, on September 25, 1964. He served the Harbor Police until September 23, 1988. John Riddle was a favorite of his grandfather's, and, with John C.'s guidance and leadership, John also became a law enforcement officer.

John Riddle and his two children, Jalen and Ayla, were given a tour of the Harbor Police facility and took a boat ride aboard the Harbor Police's newest FireStorm firefighting vessel. This was a fantastic experience for the Riddle family, as it allowed members of the third and fourth generation to experience what John's grandfather saw as he worked and served on the San Diego Bay.

JOHN C. RIDDLE. Officer John C. Riddle is pictured here in his dress uniform, in 1964. He served in the US Coast Guard before joining the Harbor Police. (Courtesy of the John Riddle.)

MEMORIES. John Riddle and his two children, Jalen & Ayla, pose with the department's newest FireStorm vessel. These boats are very different from those that John's grandfather worked on, but the duties of a Harbor Police officer are basically the same as 50 years ago. (Courtesy of John Riddle)

JALEN & AYLA. John Riddle's children pose for a photograph while visiting their great grandfather's place of work. They are in front of the San Diego Harbor Police station on Shelter Island. (Courtesy of John Riddle.)

CHRISTMAS WITH SANTA. On Christmas Day in 2010, several officers took the opportunity to take a picture with Santa Claus. From left to right are (first row) Constance Harvey, Yvette Joyner, and Michelle Rodriquez; (second row) Tracy Cain, Mr. Claus, and Jolene Seraile. (Courtesy of Michelle Rodriquez.)

AT ONE WITH NATURE. Officer Robert Glenn works alongside a pelican on the Harbor Police dock at Shelter Island. Pelicans are a normal fixture on the docks in San Diego, and officers—not wishing to disturb any local wildlife—are careful to work in harmony with them. (Courtesy of the San Diego Unified Port District.)

HARBOR POLICE FAMILY.
Pictured is the family of ducks that has made the Harbor Police station and adjacent pond their home. The San Diego Harbor Police have welcomed the ducks, which have been a fixture at the station for years. Point Loma residents and visitors love to see the ducks wandering on Shelter Island. (Courtesy of the San Diego Unified Port District.)

CALIFORNIA PEACE OFFICER MEMORIAL. In, 2013 officers attended the memorial in Sacramento, California. Harbor Police officers— along with representatives of other California law enforcement agencies—drove to Sacramento to recognize and honor California peace officers who gave their lives in the line of duty. (Courtesy of Salvador Colin.)

HARBOR POLICE PEER SUPPORT AND CRISIS INTERVENTION. Pictured are Sgt. Magda Fernandez, Cpl. Yvette Joyner, and Officer Cynthia Markley. The mission of the San Diego Harbor Police Peer Support program is to provide emotional, social, and practical support to police personnel during times of personal and professional crisis. The Crisis Intervention mission is to provide immediate emotional and practical support to victims, witnesses, and survivors involved in traumatic situations.

PEACE OFFICER MEMORIAL. Citizens and family members of fallen officers line the streets of Sacramento to honor fallen officers and welcome visiting officers from California and other states. San Diego Harbor Police representatives take part in the event on a yearly basis. (Courtesy of Salvador Colin.)

INTO THE SUNSET. The Harbor Police officers of the 21st century will continue to honor the traditions of their post by performing their duties with diligence and respect. In the next 50 years, the Harbor Police will continue to provide the citizens of San Diego with exemplary service, leadership, and integrity. This dedicated team of highly trained professionals will faithfully continue their mission to provide the highest standard of public safety and homeland security possible. (*Courtesy of David* Marshall.)

DISCOVER THOUSANDS OF LOCAL HISTORY BOOKS FEATURING MILLIONS OF VINTAGE IMAGES

Arcadia Publishing, the leading local history publisher in the United States, is committed to making history accessible and meaningful through publishing books that celebrate and preserve the heritage of America's people and places.

Find more books like this at
www.arcadiapublishing.com

Search for your hometown history, your old stomping grounds, and even your favorite sports team.

Consistent with our mission to preserve history on a local level, this book was printed in South Carolina on American-made paper and manufactured entirely in the United States. Products carrying the accredited Forest Stewardship Council (FSC) label are printed on 100 percent FSC-certified paper.

MADE IN THE USA